Is This a Career for You?

by David Brach

 HOUGHTON MIFFLIN BOSTON

ILLUSTRATION CREDITS
Joe LeMonnier

PHOTOGRAPHY CREDITS
Cover © Thinkstock/Corbis; **11** © Richard T. Nowitz/Corbis

Printed in China

ISBN 10: 0-618-90032-2
ISBN 13: 978-0-618-90032-9

23456789 NOR 16 15 14 13 12 11 10 09 08

The summer afternoon is a beautiful one at a national park in Alaska. Karl Davis looks at the thick forests and tall mountains. A moment later his cell phone rings. Karl learns that a hiker deep in the park's wilderness has been injured and needs to be flown to safety.

Karl flies a rescue helicopter. He helps people who are injured, lost, or in danger. The first thing Karl must do is find the person who needs to be rescued. To do this, he relies on detailed maps.

Karl uses topographic maps. These kinds of maps show the locations of major landforms as well as where all the land rises and falls. They show how steep slopes are, how deep canyons are, and how tall mountains are.

The map on the opposite page is a topographic map Karl uses. It is divided into squares, or a grid pattern. This grid helps Karl locate specific areas in the wilderness.

The grid helps Karl know in which direction to fly and how far he must travel. By using the grid, Karl has a much better chance of making the rescue.

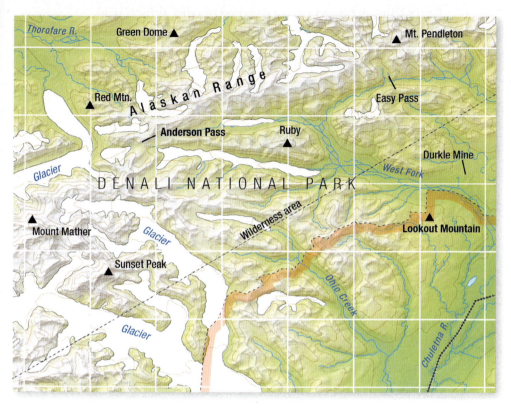

Karl knows that each square on the grid shows an area about 5 miles wide and 5 miles long.

Read·Think·Write Karl is at Lookout Mountain. The injured hiker is at Anderson Pass. About how many miles must Karl fly?

Karl's map is based on a coordinate grid, which is a pattern of uniformly spaced horizontal and vertical lines that form squares on a map. A location on a coordinate grid is called a point. A point is located by using an ordered pair, or a pair of numbers. They are called ordered pairs because the order of the two numbers matters. The number line that is used to locate a point to the left or to the right of the origin, or starting point, is called the horizontal axis, or x-axis. The number line that is used to locate a point above or below the origin, or starting point, is called the vertical axis, or y-axis.

As you study the coordinate grid on the opposite page, you can see that each axis starts at zero, like a number line.

To make his rescue, Karl must fly from one location to another.

Begin at the origin and count unit along the x-axis to find the first coordinate. Begin at the origin and count units along the y-axis to find the second coordinate. For example, the ordered pair for point A on the grid is (2, 4). To reach point A from the origin, move two units to the right and four units up.

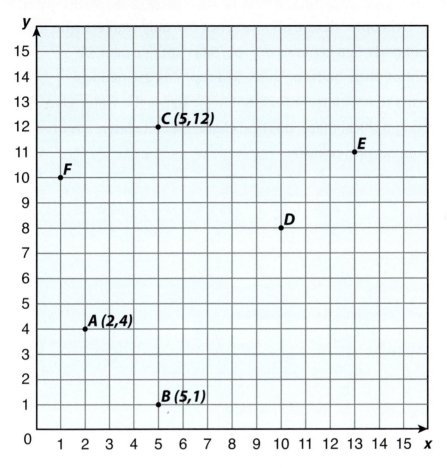

The coordinate grid can help you find the distance
between two points. For example, to get from point *B* to
point *C*, count 11 units along the *y*-axis.

Read·Think·Write Which point is at (13, 11)?

Helicopter rescue pilots are not the only workers who read grids. Sea captains do, too. Sea captains pilot, or control, large boats or ships. Sea captains use nautical charts to navigate, or find their way, across the water. Like topographical maps, nautical charts are detailed maps of lakes, oceans, or rivers.

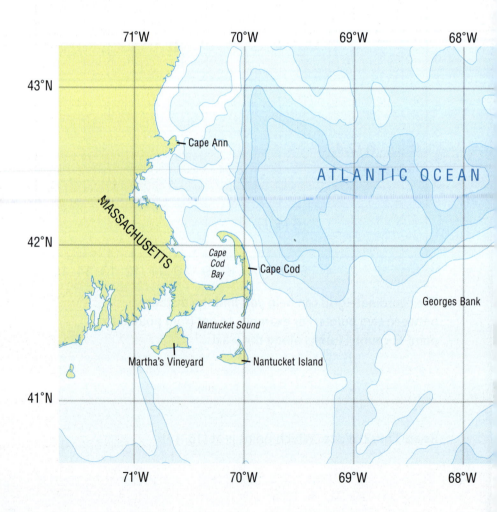

Nautical charts have lines of latitude and longitude. Latitude is the distance measured in degrees north or south of the earth's equator. Longitude is the distance measured in degrees measured east or west on earth's surface.

Like ordered pairs, lines of latitude and longitude can be used to identify specific locations on the map. A location has two numbers. The first number tells latitude, and the second number tells longitude. For example, 41°N, 69°W refers to a specific place in the Atlantic Ocean.

The captain of a fishing boat might learn that there are many fish at 43°N, 67°W. Using a nautical chart and navigational tools, captain and crew can sail to that location.

Read·Think·Write Which line of longitude runs directly through Cape Cod, Massachusetts?

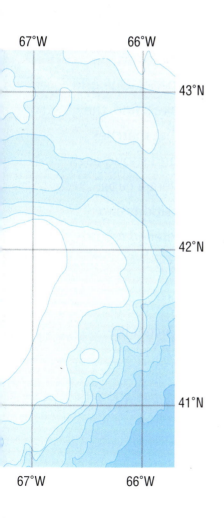

Paleontologists make and share grids. These scientists study fossils to learn about plants and animals that lived long ago.

Before paleontologists dig at a site, they use ropes and stakes to make a large grid. The grid divides the area into squares. A paleontologist digs in one square at a time.

When a fossil is dug up, important information, such as how deep it was found, could be lost. To save this information, paleontologists draw grids on paper. One grid matches the grid on the ground. As they make a find, they draw a picture of it in the square on paper that matches the square on the ground. Another kind of grid shows each square of the ground from the side, as if it were a cube. The drawings on this grid show the fossil positions and depths under the surface. This becomes a detailed record of what was found and where it was found.

Read·Think·Write Suppose a paleontologist, who was not at a dig, reads a grid record. What two locations might the paleontologist learn based on the grid?

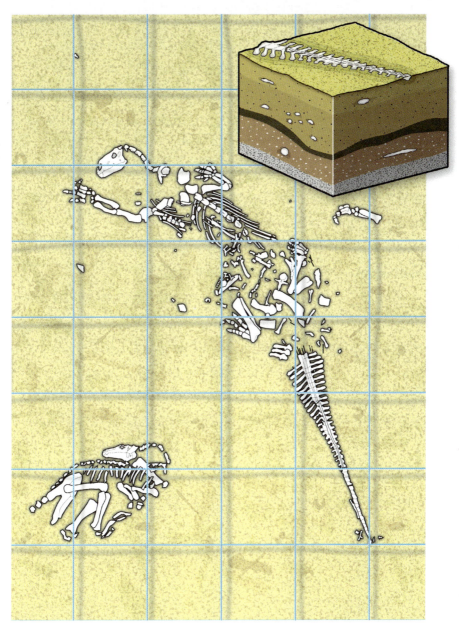

Grids help paleontologists make a detailed record of fossil locations.

Careers require specific skills. Rescue helicopter pilots must be able to fly safely. They must also know how to help people in emergencies. Sea captains must be able to pilot large boats and manage crews. Paleontologists must know how to search, keep records, make assumptions, and draw conclusions.

These careers are different, but all of them deal in some way with grids. Knowing how to understand and use grids may help you do your job well someday, too.

Learning about the everyday uses of grids can help you learn about other careers that use grids.

Careers such as a surveyor or an air traffic controller also use grids. Ask an adult in your family and friends about ways they use grids in their work.

Read·Think·Write What are some ways that you can use grids in your life now?

These paleontologists are digging within one section of a large grid.
They have a small grid laid over one area they have already dug up.

1. How many axes are on a coordinate grid?

2. What is the ordered pair for the origin of a coordinate grid?

3. What does the first number in an ordered pair tell you?

4. **Compare and Contrast** Point *G* is at (7, 5). Point *H* is at (2, 5). How many units are the two points apart?

Activity

Work with a partner. Take turns placing pattern blocks on a coordinate grid. Use letters to label where the corners of each block are located on the grid. Give the ordered pair for the location of each corner. Use a variety of blocks, such as a diamond, a trapezoid, and a hexagon.